Climate Fever

STOPPING GLOBAL WARMING

by Rachael Hanel

Content Adviser: Roberta M. Johnson, Ph.D.,
Director, Education and Outreach,
University Corporation for Atmospheric Research, Boulder, Colorado

Science Adviser: Terrence E. Young Jr., M.Ed., M.L.S.,
Jefferson Parish (Louisiana) Public School System

Reading Adviser: Alexa L. Sandmann, Ed.D., Professor of Literacy,
College and Graduate School of Education, Health, and Human Services,
Kent State University

Compass Point Books
151 Good Counsel Drive
P.O. Box 669
Mankato, MN 56002-0669

This book was manufactured with paper containing
at least 10 percent post-consumer waste.

Photographs © Alamy: Arctic Images/Ragnar Th Sigurdsson 12-13; Andrew Wilson 39; Capstone
Press: Karon Dubke 30, 46, 47, 57, 59; Corbis: epa/Alex Hofford 17, epa/Wu Hong 6, Royalty-free/
Tim Pannell 60-61, Sygma/Orban Thierry 40; Courtesy of www.Focusthenation.org 31(b); Courtesy
of letsraiseamillion.org/Jakeem Smith 48; Creatas 11(b); Energy Action Coalition/Powershift09 31(t);
FEMA News Photo: Jocelyn Augustino 23; iStockphoto: dlweis33 55, f00sion 5, GlobalP 11(t),
oversnap 21; NASA Goddard Space Flight Center (NASA-GSFC) 24; Newscom: Getty Images/AFP/
Toru Yamanaka 15; Photodisc 25; Shutterstock: Adrian Matthiassen 44, Agb 41, Anatoliy Samara
36, Andre Klaassen 9, Andy Z. 45, Armin Rose 22, egd 52, Elisei Shafer 27, Frontpage 56, Huguette
Roe 53, Ian Bracegirdle 10, James Steidl 43, Jan Martin Will 29, 50, Laurence Gough 32, Mark
Winfrey 18, Martin D. Vonka 7, maxstockphoto 4, 8, 20, 33, 42, 51, Melissa Schalke 35, michael rubin
58(t), Monkey Business Images 38, Neo Edmund 26, Oliver Hoffmann 54(all), Tony Strong 58(b),
Y.a.r.o.m.i.r. 34.

Editor: Jennifer VanVoorst
Designer: Heidi Thompson
Media Researcher: Wanda Winch
Art Director: LuAnn Ascheman-Adams
Creative Director: Joe Ewest
Editorial Director: Nick Healy
Managing Editor: Catherine Neitge

Library of Congress Cataloging-in-Publication Data
Hanel, Rachael.
  Climate fever : stopping global warming / by Rachael Hanel.
    p. cm. — (Green generation)
  Includes index.
  ISBN 978-0-7565-4246-7 (library binding)
  ISBN 978-0-7565-4291-7 (paperback)
  1. Global warming—Juvenile literature. 2. Global warming—
Environmental aspects—Juvenile literature. I. Title. II. Series.
  QC981.8.G56H36 2010
  363.738'74—dc22   2009011448

Visit Compass Point Books on the Internet at www.compasspointbooks.com
or e-mail your request to custserv@compasspointbooks.com

Contents

> " Global warming is not only the number one environmental challenge we face today, but one of the most important issues facing all of humanity. We all have to do our part to raise awareness about global warming and the problems we as a people face in promoting a sustainable environmental future for our planet."
>
> —Leonardo DiCaprio, actor and environmental activist

The Fight for the Future

introduction

Headlines blare the alarming news about global warming: Sea ice drops to some of the lowest levels ever recorded. Warmer weather patterns upset the delicate balance of Earth's food webs. Polar bears are declared an endangered species because of melting Arctic ice. All around us is proof that the planet is warming, from shrinking glaciers and intensifying storms to higher numbers of wildfires. Although the planet always has fluctuated between warm periods and cool periods, there is now a clear upward trend in Earth's temperature. Evidence

Wildfires in October and November 2007 devastated large areas of southern California.

suggests that human activity is playing a big role in how quickly the planet is heating up.

There are two ways to react to this situation. We can either sit back and do nothing, or we can make decisions and take actions that will improve Earth's health. The good news is that climate changes are causing people to think about the environment and to do positive things. More and more people are becoming active in the fight against global warming. Environmental activism started decades ago, but recently more people have been deciding that their communities and governments can make a difference.

The small steps that these people and groups have taken have already added up to big changes. California legislators passed a law requiring that the state's greenhouse gas emissions — the gases responsible for global warming — be cut 25 percent by 2020. The European Union has told its member nations to reduce carbon emissions 20 percent by 2020. The Kyoto Protocol, which calls for efforts to lower greenhouse gas emissions, has been signed by 183 countries. Chinese engineers have designed more efficient power plants. Around the world, scientists and engineers are working to develop clean-air technologies that can substitute wind and solar power for fossil

Residents of Linfen, China, wear masks to protect themselves from pollution from power plants and other sources.

fuels such as coal, oil, and natural gas, which pollute the air when burned.

Individuals are also joining the fight. Celebrities and political figures committed to fighting climate change, such as Leonardo DiCaprio and Al Gore, get public attention. Ordinary people are getting involved as well. Chances are there's someone in your community, neighborhood, or school who is making changes that will result in a healthier Earth.

You can help, too. You can start making decisions and doing things right now that will improve the planet's health for years to come. Even small steps count in the fight against global warming. Saving the planet is perhaps the most important thing we can do for ourselves and for future generations. It is a fight for the future.

By the Numbers

Energy Use in the United States Today

oil	40%
natural gas	24%
coal	23%
nuclear	8%
renewable energy	7%
electricity imports	0.1%

ethanol & biomass	3.6%
hydroelectric	2.4%
geothermal	0.35%
wind	0.3%
solar	0.08%

What Is Global Warming?

chapter 1

By now the concept of global warming is familiar to almost everyone. The news media, politicians, and concerned citizens have drawn attention to the problem for many years. We're bombarded with terms such as "greenhouse gases," "carbon footprint," and "alternative energy." But what exactly is global warming? And what can be done to tackle the problem?

A giant greenhouse:

Global warming is the rise in Earth's temperature that occurs when certain gases in the atmosphere trap the sun's heat rather than letting it escape into space. About half of the sun's energy reaches Earth's surface. It heats the land and water. Some of that heat bounces back up into the atmosphere in the form of invisible infrared rays. Under normal conditions, some of the reflected heat is trapped in the atmosphere. The atmosphere acts like the glass walls of a greenhouse, making the planet warm enough to support life.

But when too much heat is trapped in the atmosphere, the result is higher global temperatures. Certain gases, known as greenhouse gases, are to blame for this excess heat. Most of these gases occur naturally in the atmosphere and have been around since Earth's formation.

Some of the gases in Earth's atmosphere are increasing because of human activity, causing global warming.

However, industries, other businesses, and vehicles have greatly increased the amount of greenhouse gases in the atmosphere.

The most common greenhouse gas is carbon dioxide. Carbon dioxide accounts for 80 percent of all greenhouse gas emissions. Carbon dioxide is released into the air when we burn fossil fuels such as coal, oil, and natural gas. We use these fuels to heat our homes, power our vehicles, and run our factories. When we burn down forests, carbon dioxide from trees is released in the smoke.

The greenhouse gases methane and nitrous oxide are found in smaller amounts in the atmosphere, but their levels are also rising

Power plants that burn fossil fuels release the greenhouse gas carbon dioxide into the atmosphere.

because of human activity. Liquid manure pits on large cattle and pig farms release methane into the air, and so do garbage landfills. Nitrous oxide comes from fertilizers and the burning of fossil fuels. Other greenhouse gases don't exist in nature and are created through industrial processes.

A natural cycle?

Since 1860 Earth's overall temperature has increased about 1 degree Fahrenheit (0.6 degrees Celsius). That may not seem like much, but spread over the entire planet, a difference of even a few tenths of a degree

Landfills are engineered to keep contaminants out of the soil, but they release methane into the air.

can cause big changes in ocean currents and plant and animal habitats.

The scientific data clearly indicate that the planet is warming. However, data also show that Earth has warmed before. It has cooled before, too, in a number of "ice ages." So are we just experiencing a natural cycle, or is something more going on?

One way to answer this question is by looking at carbon dioxide levels throughout history. Ice

Scientists use core samples to measure the changes in ice's carbon dioxide levels over time.

samples in Antarctica hold clues as to what the atmosphere was like long ago. Tiny gas bubbles have been trapped in the ice, and those bubbles contain carbon dioxide, which scientists can measure. A graph showing carbon dioxide levels from several thousand years ago until today looks like a hockey stick lying on its

Consider the Source

For all the people compiling evidence that supports the presence of global warming, there are some people who question whether it's actually happening. Some question whether Earth is really heating up. Others agree that the planet is warming, but they doubt that human activity is responsible. Some think that even if humans are responsible for global warming, the predicted consequences have been exaggerated.

Scientists and researchers who study the issue are in the best position to determine what global warming is and what is causing it. They often publish their findings in journals that go through a rigorous review and editing process. One study found that out of a large sample of journal articles addressing global warming, not one disagreed with the consensus that global warming is happening and that human activity is a cause.

Doubt is likely caused by the fact that most people get their information from the news media, not scientific journals. The news media usually try to portray both sides of an issue, so those opposed to evidence of global warming are quoted. Some global warming skeptics are employed by or connected with oil, coal, or utility companies. Acknowledging global warming could lead to restrictions on their activities and hurt their profits.

There's a lot of information about global warming, and it's important to look at the source. Who's behind the information—an independent, scientific, neutral source, or a large oil company?

side. The line was flat for thousands of years, but it has skyrocketed upward in the past 150 years. This increase coincides with the flourishing of the Industrial Revolution. Today carbon dioxide levels are much higher than at any other time in history. The evidence points to the conclusion that human activity is to blame for the high rise in greenhouse gases, and therefore, Earth's rising temperatures.

If nothing is done to reduce greenhouse gas emissions, scientists predict, there will be far more significant global changes because of warming in the 21st century than were seen in the 20th century.

The Kyoto Protocol:

Countries around the world are taking steps to reduce greenhouse gas emissions. The leading document in which most countries have agreed to reduce emissions

Representatives from about 170 countries wrote the Kyoto Protocol in December 1997.

is the Kyoto Protocol. In 1997 world leaders gathered in Kyoto, Japan, to discuss the problem of rising greenhouse gas emissions and their role in global warming. The leaders decided that it was critical to work together to reduce greenhouse gases, because what happens in one country affects the entire world.

The goal of the agreement was to reduce greenhouse gases by 5 percent of 1990 levels by 2012. The Kyoto Protocol went into effect in 2005, and countries that ratified it have agreed to adhere to those standards. A country that falls short of that target has to make up the shortfall in later years and reduce emissions by an

Greenhouse Gas Giant

Although China is the leading emitter of greenhouse gases, Americans produce far more greenhouse gases, on a per-person basis, than the Chinese. In part that's because China's population of more than 1 billion people is about four times that of the United States. In addition, much of the world's manufacturing takes place in China, where U.S. and European countries have set up factories. Because China produces so much of what we wear, eat, and otherwise use, China is, in a sense, emitting greenhouse gases that rightly belong to much of the rest of the world.

extra 30 percent.

So far 183 countries have ratified the protocol. If every country hits the target, greenhouse gas emissions will decrease. But although the United States releases 30 percent of the world's greenhouse gases, it has yet to ratify the agreement. It has refused to do so for two reasons. First, the U.S. government disagrees with a clause in the protocol that exempts developing countries from having to reduce their admissions. American leaders argue that China and India are still classified as developing countries, but they are fast becoming industrial giants. In fact China has surpassed the United States as the leading producer of greenhouse gases. Some U.S. government leaders have worried that following the protocol would strain the U.S. economy. But the 2009 change in presidential administration may bring

The Chinese city of Hong Kong's smog-clouded skyline results from the pollution caused by burning fossil fuels.

changes to the U.S. policy on the Kyoto Protocol as well. For example, in 2009 the Environmental Protection Agency declared carbon dioxide and five other greenhouse gases to be pollutants. This led the way to regulating them for the first time in U.S. history.

Independent efforts:

Many cities and states have taken their own steps to reduce emissions. In 2006 Governor Arnold Schwarzenegger of California signed into law the state's Global Warming Solutions Act. It was the first law in the United States to put a cap on emissions. The goal is to reduce emissions to 1990 levels, a 25 percent cut, by 2020. California aims to further reduce emissions to 80 percent below 1990 levels by 2050. Before the law was passed, California alone produced more carbon dioxide than all but 11 countries.

In the United States, more laws each year place higher importance on reducing global warming. Politicians propose laws when it's obvious that most of the public is concerned about global warming and wants to see policies that will reduce it. In the 110th Congress (2007–2008), senators and representatives introduced 235 bills, resolutions, and amendments that addressed some aspect of global warming. Not all of these became law, but this was more action—by far—than in any other previous congressional session. Vocal public opinion is bringing more attention to the topic and producing results.

Making the Cut

Several American cities have taken it upon themselves to cut down on carbon emissions. In 2006 more than 80 percent of voters in Berkeley, California, approved Measure G, which pledges to cut the city's emissions 80 percent by 2050. In 2007 Seattle Mayor Greg Nickels launched the U.S. Mayors Climate Protection Agreement. In it more than 700 American mayors agreed to meet or beat the Kyoto Protocol goals in their communities. Even the largest city in the United States is taking notice. PlanNYC 2030 includes measures to make New York City more environmentally responsible by 2030. Among the goals: reducing emissions by 30 percent and having the best air quality of any large city in the United States.

"It is important for all of us to take note of the changes occurring in our environment and our role in that process. Each of us can do something, change some of our daily patterns, to secure the planet and stem global warming."
    —Wangari Maathai, environmental activist and Nobel Prize winner

Extreme Effects

chapter 2

Every region of Earth is vulnerable to global warming's effects. Mountains, valleys, oceans, and tundras are all changing. Rising temperatures and sea levels affect the land and the water, as well as the plants and animals that live there. Sometimes the changes are barely noticeable, but at other times the differences are dramatic.

Take glaciers and polar ice caps, for example. In the African country of Tanzania, the majestic Mount Kilimanjaro was once covered with large expanses of ice and snow. Today

The ice cap atop Tanzania's Mount Kilimanjaro
is shrinking because of global warming.

the mountain's ice cap has shrunk greatly. Glaciers used to cover the Alps and the Andes, but today those rivers of ice are shrinking dramatically, leaving behind barren ground littered with rocks and mud.

Rising waters: In our oceans, rising water levels threaten animals and humans. Sea levels have risen 4 to 8 inches (10 to 20 centimeters) over the past 100 years. Higher temperatures cause water to expand in volume, and melting ice from the poles also contributes to rising sea levels. About 40 percent of the world's 6.5 billion people live within 60 miles (97 kilometers) of a coast. This puts a

Melting polar ice is a cause of concern
for many environmental scientists.

great number of people
at risk for major flooding.
Along many coastal areas the
land is at or near sea level.

Extreme weather:

Warmer water also has been
linked to extreme weather.
Warm water increases the
moisture in the air, which
leads to stronger storms. In
recent years, storms around
the globe seem to have
intensified. In 2004 Florida
was hit by four powerful
hurricanes, and Japan
received the brunt of 10
typhoons, a record number.
In 2005 Hurricane Katrina
devastated New Orleans,
Louisiana, with high winds
and, when the levees broke,
massive flooding.

New Orleans is mostly below sea level. When the levees failed, the city held water from the storm like a bowl.

Changing climate:

On Earth's landmasses, warming has noticeably affected the northern-most latitudes and highest altitudes. Fewer cold and snowy days and more warm and dry days are recorded. Since satellites started taking pictures of Earth in the 1960s, scientists have noticed that snow cover has decreased in area worldwide about 10 percent. Higher temperatures also mean that more precipitation is falling as rain rather than as snow. Rainfalls are heavier and more devastating than in the past. Europe, North and South America, and Africa all report sharp increases in the number of floods in the past 50 years. However, the rise in overall temperature produces widely different conditions in different areas. Traditionally wet areas such as tropical rain forests, for example, are now receiving less rainfall.

Changing habitats:

Perhaps the most dramatic differences can be seen in the polar regions. The polar ice caps, as well as Greenland's glaciers, are shrinking rapidly. As a result, the animals that live in these remote and challenging environments are suddenly in real danger of losing their homes.

In the Arctic Ocean, the amount of sea ice shrinks

The Antarctic ice cap shrank dramatically when parts of the Larsen Ice Shelf collapsed in early 2002.

more each year. Some ice melts every summer, but it refreezes in the winter. However, 2007 and 2008 had the least sea ice formation since 1979. Each year more ice is lost in the summer and not recovered in the winter. This puts Arctic creatures such as the polar bear at risk of extinction. Polar bears are good swimmers. But as ice sheets grow thinner and break up, they must swim farther to hunt and migrate. More than a quarter of them have died in the last few years, and they are increasingly endangered. Recent

Global warming is endangering animals such as the polar bear by changing their habitat faster than they can adapt.

reports predict that 30 percent of polar bears will be lost by 2050.

Animals that live in Antarctica's cold, barren wastes are at risk as well. This continent is the single largest ice sheet on the planet. However, global warming is causing huge chunks of ice to break away from the mainland. This is changing the habitat of the several species of penguins that live there. One species, the emperor penguin, is dramatically declining in numbers. In the last 50 years, scientists estimate, the emperor penguin population has decreased 70 percent, probably because global warming is changing the animals' environment.

Animals in tropical areas are also affected by rising temperatures.

Animals at Risk

The polar bear and emperor penguin are just two animals at risk of extinction because of global warming. Here are some others:

- caribou
- monarch butterfly
- arctic fox
- leopard seal
- red-breasted goose
- harlequin frog
- wattled crane
- Adelie penguin
- gray-headed albatross
- bowhead whale

Check It

Coral reefs are especially sensitive to the effects of global warming. These living underwater cities are made up of the protective exoskeletons of billions of tiny organisms. Coral reefs provide underwater havens for diverse ocean life, but warmer waters are killing the reefs in large numbers.

Taking steps: Although the effects of global warming on the planet are noticeable, we have the power and technology to reduce or eliminate them, should we

Coral reefs cover less than 1 percent of Earth's surface, but they are home to 25 percent of all marine fish species.

Global Warming 101

Who better to publicize the shifting Arctic climate than someone who's seen the changes firsthand? Noted polar explorer Will Steger traveled to the North Pole by dogsled in 1986, part of a team that was the first to reach the pole since the 1909 Robert Peary expedition. Since then he's explored all parts of the Arctic. Steger has seen that the sea ice is becoming thinner and, in some places, disappearing altogether.

To make others aware of his observations, Steger created the Will Steger Foundation in 2006. One of the foundation's programs is called Global Warming 101. The program's goal is to raise public awareness of the effects of global warming on the planet. Global Warming 101 uses the Internet to help people make informed decisions about climate change and to inspire individuals to take action.

choose to do so. The process will be slow. Ocean levels will not drop overnight. Glaciers and sea ice will not suddenly reappear. Policies that reduce carbon emissions, such as the Kyoto Protocol, will help in the long run. For now, however, there are steps people can take to lessen the effects on plants, animals, and water, as well as on themselves.

The U.S. government is already making some adjustments. In 2008 the polar bear was listed as a threatened species—the first animal to be put on the list solely because of global warming's effects. This listing requires the government to develop policies that protect the animal's habitat. The U.S. Fish and Wildlife Service is considering adding 10 penguin species to the list of animals protected by the federal Endangered Species Act. Individuals can create change as well, either through the political system or on their own. Policy changes come through governing bodies, such as school boards, city councils, state legislatures, or the U.S. Congress. People who are concerned about climate change can learn more about political candidates and decide which ones are committed to reducing greenhouse gas emissions and working to protect land,

Get to know people in your local government who can help you make the changes you want.

water, and animals. They can write to policymakers and speak up at meetings of government bodies.

Speaking up: Individuals are also speaking up on their own to call attention to the effects of global warming. All around the planet, young people are teaming up to educate others about climate change. In 2007, for example, college students from across the United States met in Washington, D.C., for the first Power Shift conference. Power Shift was the first global warming summit entirely composed of young people. The students, many of whom already had experience at the local and state levels raising global-warming awareness, gathered to share ideas. The group pledged to take nationwide action. Power Shift is looking for more young people to join the group and tell others about its efforts.

Focus the Nation is a network of college students eager to spread the word about stopping global warming. On January 31, 2008, the organization held a "teach in" that connected campuses across the nation. Organizers estimate that 1 million people took part in the event.

With today's technology, it's becoming easier than ever to find like-minded people who are committed to stopping global warming. A simple Internet search can provide the sites of many organizations in which people can get involved. The Web sites offer tips for reducing your effect on the environment, and they provide examples of how to take action and spread the word. The Internet, social networking sites, and text messaging allow information to be delivered to more people, and faster, than ever before.

Working green:

People who want to make a difference can combine their passion for activism with a career. More and more young people are choosing careers in environmental studies, and more colleges and universities are offering programs and degrees in that field. The number of "green collar" jobs that focus on the environment is steadily growing. Cascadia Community College near Seattle, Washington, recently began offering a two-year Environmental Technologies and Sustainable Practices program, which prepares students for environmental careers. Other programs around the country specialize in coastal management, clean-energy technology, and creating and installing solar panels. It's becoming easier than ever to make a career out of climate change activism. Creating change now will help prevent some of the dire consequences in store for Earth if nothing is done to cool the planet's fever.

There are many fields of study you can pursue if you're interested in helping the environment.

"It is our duty, our responsibility, to ensure that our children, our children's children, and all the generations that follow have the opportunity to experience these treasures we so often take for granted. Let us all come together as one collective unit in an effort to sustain our planet as we know it."
—Carson Palmer, National Football League player

Changing the Forecast

chapter 3

We're already seeing what global warming is doing to Earth's resources. There are two options before us. We can do nothing and let the harmful effects worsen, or we can do something to reverse the effects. Fortunately millions of people are choosing to do something. Some choose to drive less, sign petitions, donate money, or educate the public. Each day more and more people are joining the fight against climate change. It's a good thing, too—scientists predict that increased warming will cause irreversible damage to the planet if nothing is done to stop it.

A dire prediction: The picture scientists paint of Earth's future is bleak. According to the Intergovernmental Panel on Climate Change, 20 to 30 percent of animal species worldwide are at risk of extinction if nothing changes. Droughts are expected to affect more regions. At the same time, rainfall in other regions is predicted to become heavier and more localized, increasing the risk of flash flooding.

If nothing is done to reverse the trend, polar ice will continue to melt—with alarming consequences. Scientists estimate that if the ice on Greenland and in Antarctica melted, sea levels would rise by 23 feet (7 m).

In extreme drought, parched soil cracks and separates.

By 2080 millions of people would be displaced each year because of coastal flooding. But the continental coasts would not be the only areas destroyed by rising sea levels. Many low-lying islands around the world would simply disappear under the waves. Most of the Florida Keys would be gone, for example.

Climate change could harm human health as well. One-sixth of the world's population lives in areas where the water supply comes from glaciers and snow cover. When glaciers and snowcaps retreat, water supplies decline. Droughts, floods, and

The Ganges River, which flows through India, is fed by a glacier that is rapidly retreating.

changing growing seasons may make staple crops such as corn and wheat harder to grow. As a result, more people would be at risk of malnutrition. Extreme weather is expected to cause widespread deaths. Poor air quality because of increased emissions would contribute to more respiratory illnesses. Higher temperatures would let diseases spread to new areas more easily.

Mitigation and adaptation: The right choice is clear: We must act. Already around the world, politicians, scientists, and individuals young and old are finding ways to protect Earth's future. This can be done in two ways. One process is called mitigation.

Mitigation lessens the effects of global warming. For example, reducing greenhouse gases through policies such as the Kyoto Protocol is one way to mitigate the problem.

The other process is adaptation, which means making a change in response to a situation. Earth is getting warmer, so plants, animals, and humans are adapting in many ways. Some animals and plants adapt by finding cooler weather at higher elevations or more northern latitudes. Humans adapt by building stronger houses in coastal areas or constructing solid levees that lessen the chance of flooding. Farmers adapt by adjusting the type of crops they grow. Warmer weather can mean a longer growing season. This can help increase yields, and farmers can bring in new income by growing new crops.

The Carbon Market

One attempt to mitigate the effects of global warming is the cap-and-trade approach, otherwise known as the carbon market. In cap-and-trade, companies are issued permits that allow them to emit a fixed amount of greenhouse gases into the atmosphere. Companies that reduce greenhouse gas emissions can make money by selling their extra emission allowance to companies that cannot meet the requirements. Companies that do not meet the target are penalized by being required to buy extra permits. This approach gives companies a financial incentive to reduce emissions as much as possible.

The first carbon market opened in the United States in September 2008. Ten states in the Northeast banded together to form a regional market. Other regions are following this example. The Western Climate Initiative is composed of seven Western states and four Canadian provinces. In 2008 the group announced plans for its own cap-and-trade system.

Scientists and policymakers believe that mitigation and adaptation must occur together. Simply responding to a situation through adaptation is not enough. Something must be done to try to change the problem through mitigation. However, mitigation can take many years to become effective. In the meantime, we must find ways to adapt to a warmer world.

Making a difference:

Many countries are taking steps to help their populations survive a changing climate. In the Netherlands, where more than 10 million of the nation's 16 million people live below sea level, officials are using strong measures to protect the land from rising water. A panel recommended that the government spend $144 billion in the next 100 years to expand dunes and strengthen dikes.

Individuals can do something as simple as getting on a bike to run errands and to go to school instead of getting in a car. In several states, students are encouraged to ride their bikes to school. The city of Minneapolis, Minnesota, produced a 36-page guide called "Minneapolis Safe Routes to School" to

Be part of the solution: Bike to school, if you can.

encourage more bicycle ridership. Sometimes it takes just a simple change to encourage more ridership. For example, after officials at South High School in Minneapolis installed new bike racks and showed students how to properly lock their bikes, ridership increased from 30 students a day to 150.

Often it's young people who are energetically trying to make a difference. One young woman in San Francisco, California, has created a community garden in the middle of an urban area. Maya Donelson has partnered with Glide Church to make a garden on the church's rooftop. The project, called Graze the Roof, makes fresh produce available in an area with little food production. The locally grown food helps eliminate

Maya Donelson's Graze the Roof project offers gardening classes and workshops for youths and adults.

A Politician for the Planet

Perhaps more than anyone else, former U.S. Vice President Al Gore has brought worldwide attention to the problem of global warming. As a member of Congress in the 1970s and 1980s, Gore fought for policies that would combat climate change. In 1992 he published *Earth in the Balance*, a book that encouraged environmental responsibility. In 2006 he released a documentary film titled *An Inconvenient Truth*. In it Gore outlined the evidence of climate change, described how it's affecting Earth, and told what people can do about it. Gore, along with a U.N. panel on climate change, won the 2007 Nobel Peace Prize for their efforts in spreading the word about global warming.

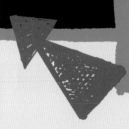

greenhouse gases produced by trucks hauling produce into the city. Reliance on locally grown crops helps reduce the demand for crops grown elsewhere. Urban food production can play a big role in feeding city populations, especially if predictions about decreasing crop production around the world come true.

At Lafayette College in Easton, Pennsylvania, student Jennifer Bell designed a system in which uneaten food from the campus dining hall is composted, not thrown away. Food scraps are mixed with leaves and grass, and after two weeks, the mixture can be used as a rich topsoil for growing plants. The school's goal is to compost all leftover food from the dining hall. The college also has started a program called "What Can I Do?" to encourage students to develop environmentally conscious practices.

The ominous outlook for global warming's effects becomes a little brighter when we realize that governments and individuals are trying to create change. Action often has a snowball effect. One country makes laws to reduce emissions, and other countries follow suit. One person joins in the fight against global warming, then another, and then another. For many years, no one took any action. Now we're witnessing an exciting time in history. People are taking climate change seriously, and they are willing to do something about it.

> "The good news is we know what to do. The good news is we have everything we need now to respond to the challenge of global warming. We have all the technologies we need; more are being developed. And as they become available and become more afford-able when produced in scale, they will make it easier to respond. But we should not wait, we cannot wait, we must not wait."
> —Al Gore, environmental activist, Nobel Prize winner, and former vice president of the United States

Technological Solutions

chapter 4

Since global warming is caused by increased amounts of greenhouse gases in the air, the logical way to combat climate change is to reduce greenhouse gas emissions. Thankfully, technology exists to do just that, and it is getting better each year. But as with any complicated global problem, the switch to cleaner technology and fuels can't happen overnight. People and industries are used to their old habits. Despite the damage that continuing along this same path will cause future generations, some people and indus-tries are actively working against the changes needed to reduce the global warming threat. But the winds of change are blowing. People are becoming increasingly willing to alter their behaviors in order to help the planet.

To meet the Kyoto Protocol reduction goals in the next couple of decades means that technological solutions must be put into action today. Many of these solutions involve a switch to renewable energy.

Our dependence on nonrenewable energy, such as oil, has played a large part in creating the climate crisis. Nonrenewable fuels are those with limited supplies. The planet contains only a certain amount of fossil fuels. Eventually they will run out. Perhaps worse, fossil fuels produce greenhouse gases when burned.

Wind, which can be transformed into electricity by turbines, is one of several sources of renewable energy.

Renewable energy:

Renewable energy does not run out. Renewable energy comes from a variety of sources, including the sun, wind, water, and plants. Scientists are working on ways to develop power from these renewable sources, which can supply what is known as clean, nonpolluting energy.

Solar power is a popular source of clean and safe renewable energy. This type of energy comes from the sun. Solar panels can be placed on towers or roofs to absorb the sun's light and convert it to electricity.

Wind can be used to create electrical power as well. The wind turns blades on giant turbines, which convert the wind's mechanical power into electricity. Groups of turbines, called wind farms, are growing in

Solar panels are angled to maximize the amount of energy they can capture from the sun.

Hydroelectric dams convert the movement of water into clean energy.

number all across the world. The five countries leading the way in wind power production are Germany, the United States, Spain, India, and China.

Water is another source of renewable energy. As with wind power, moving water from rivers or tides turns turbines, which create electricity. Water is the leading renewable energy source used by electric utilities to generate electric power.

Another promising alternative energy source takes advantage of the heat deep inside the planet. Geothermal power is created by drilling down to reach underground reserves of superheated water. The water is brought to the surface, where its steam is used to turn turbines, which generate electricity.

Scientists are looking at ways to use renewable energy

in vehicles. Already hybrid cars, which run on a combination of electricity and gasoline, are becoming a popular choice among consumers. Researchers also are exploring options that could reduce drivers' dependence upon gasoline and oil. Ethanol-based fuels are available, and more cars are using this fuel, which is made from corn and other plants. For larger vehicles that normally run on diesel fuel, such as trucks, buses, and tractors, biodiesel options are being developed. Biodiesel is a plant-based fuel, usually made from soybean oil. Hydrogen is also being explored as a clean, renewable source of energy.

Saving energy: The energy efficiency of everything from lightbulbs to buildings is getting more attention. Something that is energy-efficient uses the least energy possible to provide power. U.S. consumers have recently been given the option of using compact fluorescent lightbulbs. CFLs use less energy and last longer than traditional bulbs. It's estimated that if every U.S. household replaced one ordinary lightbulb with a CFL, enough energy would be saved to power 3 million homes for a year. Doing this would also save $600 million in energy costs and would reduce greenhouse gas emissions as much as taking 800,000 cars off the roads. In the construction industry, more homes, offices, and schools are being built using "green" designs. These buildings are energy-efficient and produce less waste and less greenhouse gases.

Share information on global warming with your classmates, and see what a difference you can make.

Bringing attention:

Scientists and engineers are creating and applying these technologies, but it's often the younger generation that is bringing attention to the problems and the solutions. Young people across the United States and the world are getting on their bikes, circulating petitions, and asking government and business leaders for greener practices. They hope to get everyone to play a part in fighting global warming.

In the summer of 2008, 14-year-old Liza Stoner of Minneapolis hopped on her bike and rode all the way to the U.S. Capitol in Washington, D.C.—a distance of 1,585 miles (2,551 km). Once there, Liza delivered a petition signed by 1,200 people to

Minnesota Senator Amy Klobuchar. The petition asked Congress to pass a law offering tax incentives and credits to companies that produce and use electric cars.

In Atlanta, Georgia, the Let's Raise a Million project is the brainchild of Tony Anderson, a student at Morehouse College. Anderson is trying to get 1 million compact fluores-cent lightbulbs and install them in the homes of people who might not otherwise be able to afford them. The switch to CFLs will save the residents money while reducing the homes' environ-mental impact.

Liz Veazey has been working on renewable energy action for many years. In 2003, while she was a student at the University of North Carolina, she pushed the

Let's Raise a Million volunteers collected CFLs to distribute to people with low incomes.

A High-Stakes Tug-of-War

Like many important problems, global warming has become a political issue. At times there seems to be a tug-of-war taking place between those who want to do something quickly about climate change and those who don't think it is a serious problem.

It is up to the government to make laws and regulations to fight global warming. But fighting global warming means that we as individuals must change our lifestyles. It means that we need to buy less gasoline and power our homes and businesses with renewable energy instead of fossil fuels. Companies that supply nonrenewable energy are often multi-billion-dollar businesses with a lot of power in the political world. If people buy less of what these companies sell, the companies could lose money. So the companies try to persuade politicians to not make laws and regulations that would harm their business.

Some politicians refuse to take a stand on global warming in the hope of not angering anyone. Voters have to demand that the fight against global warming be made a top priority. If the voices of voters are not heard, politicians might be tempted to stand by and do nothing. Individuals must band together to persuade politicians to enact change for university's leaders to power the campus with renewable energy. Money from increased student fees went into a fund to buy power from clean sources. Thanks to Veazey's dedication, UNC was the first campus in the southeastern United States to obtain some of its energy from renewable resources.

Organizations are starting to take notice and to give grants to encourage young people to continue their environmental activism. For example, in 2008, Focus the Nation, along with the Clif Bar company, awarded three grants to youth activists who were making a difference in halting global warming.

Jesse Hough, a student at the University of Oregon, received one of the grants. He developed a plan for a neighborhood energy district. Under the plan, solar panels at Sunnyside Environmental School in Portland would

heat water, which would be piped to nearby houses and businesses to supply hot water and heat. The school's old furnace would be replaced with a biodiesel generator. Hough is also co-founder of Cascade Climate Network, an organization of students in the northwestern United States that is committed to creating a healthier world.

Working together, people young and old can reduce the causes and effects of global warming and make our planet a healthier place for all living things.

"This is the moment when we must come together to save this planet. Let us resolve that we will not leave our children a world where the oceans rise and famine spreads and terrible storms devastate our lands. Let us resolve that all nations—including my own—will act with seriousness of purpose, and reduce the carbon we send into the atmosphere. This is the moment to give our children back their future. This is the moment to stand as one."
—Barack Obama, 44th president of the United States

Take Action!

chapter 5

By educating yourself, you're already taking an important first step in the fight against global warming. Knowledge is power. People who want to take action about global warming need to learn as much as they can about the subject. The more you know, the more you can spread the word to others.

Do as much as you can to change the way you live. The biggest actions start with small steps. In this big world, one thing you can control is your own behavior and actions.

Shrink your footprint:

For starters, try to reduce your carbon footprint. This is the amount of greenhouse gas generated by a person, organization, or location. When a car is driven, the burning of the fuel releases carbon dioxide. Gas and coal used for heat also produce greenhouse gases, as does food production. You can live a life in which you create a large carbon footprint, or you can try to reduce your impact on the planet. To measure your footprint, you can use one of the many carbon footprint calculators on the Internet.

Individual changes don't have to be drastic. It's estimated that if countries reduced their carbon dioxide emissions by 3 percent each year from now until 2050, global emissions would be cut by nearly 95 percent.

The rise in the number of cars worldwide has increased emissions and contributed to global warming.

What does a 3 percent reduction mean for one person? For someone who drives 1,000 miles (1,600 km) per month, a 3 percent reduction means driving 30 fewer miles (48 km).

Bag the bags: The list of ways you can save energy by making tiny changes is endless. Giving up plastic bags is one example. Producing plastic bags uses energy and releases greenhouse gases into the atmosphere. Many bags end up in landfills, where they contribute to the release of methane, a greenhouse gas. So take your own cloth bags when you go shopping. If you forget and leave your bag at home, you might find that you don't need a bag after all. If you buy just one compact disc or book, resist the temptation to

Every year Americans throw away 100 billion plastic bags—most of which have only been used once.

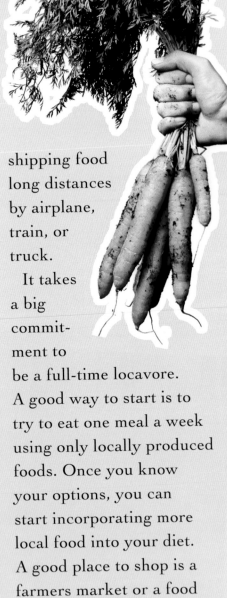

take a plastic bag. If you must take one, try to reuse it at home. They make great liners for garbage cans and cat litter boxes. Or tuck one in your backpack to use as a makeshift head wrap if you're caught in an unexpected downpour.

Eat local: Another smart way to reduce your carbon footprint is to buy locally grown food. A movement that is quickly gaining popularity is known as the "locavore" movement. An herbivore eats only plants, an omnivore eats meat and plants, and a locavore is a person who buys food produced nearby. A locavore not only supports the local economy, but also reduces the large carbon footprint associated with shipping food long distances by airplane, train, or truck.

It takes a big commitment to be a full-time locavore. A good way to start is to try to eat one meal a week using only locally produced foods. Once you know your options, you can start incorporating more local food into your diet. A good place to shop is a farmers market or a food cooperative, a store whose customers are also owners.

You might even want to plant your own garden.

If you live in a city without garden space, find out whether there's a community garden in your town. If not, think about starting one.

Wherever you shop, try to buy the food that has the least amount of packaging. Instead of buying individually wrapped snacks, buy them in bulk and put them into your own reusable containers. Instead of individual cans or bottles of juices or soft drinks, buy them in larger containers and put your drink in a bottle or travel mug that you can refill again and again.

Farmers markets are great places to shop for organic, locally grown food.

Limit meat: If you eat meat, try to reduce the amount you consume. Raising cattle and processing beef creates a large quantity of carbon dioxide. Forests are being razed to provide more grazing land for cattle. It takes less land and produces less carbon dioxide to grow plants, some of which can provide the same amount of protein that is in red meat.

Cattle graze in a field recently cleared out of the Brazilian rain forest.

Ditch the Bottled Water, Save the Planet

The plastic water bottle is a mainstay in American society. We turn to these bottles because we like to drink water that is fresh, cool, and convenient. Many of us recycle our bottles when we're done with them, and some people even reuse them by filling them up with tap water. While this is much better than simply throwing them away, it would be best for global warming to not buy bottled water at all.

Most water bottles are made of plastic, which is made from oil. Most of the bottles are produced at plants that operate using power from oil or coal. In addition, it's estimated that it takes slightly more than three quarts (three liters) of water to produce one quart (one liter) of bottled water. It takes a vast amount of energy to transport the bottles to stores, and also to collect the bottles for recycling and to recycle them.

A better choice is to buy your own water container, which you can fill again and again with tap water. Regular tap water, especially in most metropolitan areas, usually tastes just as good as bottled water. In fact, some bottled water comes from city water supplies. The only difference is that bottled water costs you—and the planet—a whole lot more.

GO DEEP

Travel green: How you get yourself from place to place also affects global warming. Before you hop in a car, ask yourself whether you could walk, bike, or use public transportation. If you must take a car, try to combine errands to make your car use as efficient as possible. Set up carpools to get to school or events. If you must use a car, you can increase its efficiency. Slow down. Efficiency decreases rapidly for every mile per hour you drive over 55 mph (88 kph). Keep your family's car properly tuned and maintained. Don't let

Public transportation, such as light rail, helps keep cars off the road, thereby reducing emissions.

the air pressure in the tires get too low. Don't run the engine if you're waiting for a friend or for a train to pass, or just to warm up the car in the winter.

Find others: Once you've become informed and have taken steps to reduce your energy consumption, find other people who are committed to doing the same thing. See what resources are available in your community or school. Are there scientists and activists who live near you? Perhaps neighbors and friends have experience in community organizing, public speaking, or public policymaking. Get to know people on your school board, city council, or county board. Modern technology makes it easier than ever to find others

Talk with your friends and neighbors, and encourage them to join you in the fight against global warming.

dedicated to fighting global warming. Use the Internet or post flyers around school to form a group. Social networking sites such as Facebook list a variety of global warming-related groups that you can join.

But it all comes down to this: To make an impact, people must be willing to change their lifestyles. With dedicated politicians, scientists, and individuals focusing on global warming, the prospect for changing

Get together with your friends and take action—any action—to help protect the planet.

old habits looks good. Of course, there's much more that needs to be done. In order to make a differ- ence, everyone will have to work together toward a common goal. More than ever, though, it's becoming easier—and more impor- tant—for each person to make small changes that result in big rewards.

Glossary

alternative energy—energy source, such as solar or wind power, that can replace fossil fuels without contributing to carbon dioxide emissions

atmosphere—blanket of gases that surrounds a planet

biomass—natural products and waste that can be made into usable energy

carbon footprint—measure of the amount of carbon dioxide produced by a person, organization, or location at a given time

compost—organic wastes that are allowed to decompose naturally

emissions—substances released into the air

fossil fuels—fuels, including coal, oil, and natural gas, that are made from the remains of ancient organisms

glaciers—large masses of slowly moving ice

greenhouse effect—warming that happens when certain gases in Earth's atmosphere trap heat and thereby warm Earth's surface

greenhouse gases—gases in a planet's atmosphere that trap heat energy from the sun

infrared rays—heat rays; a form of radiation similar to visible light that is given off by all warm objects

malnutrition—condition in which the body receives too little food

precipitation—water falling from the sky as rain, sleet, hail, or snow

tundras—treeless plains found in the Arctic and at high altitudes

typhoons—hurricanes in the western Pacific Ocean

Investigate Further

MORE BOOKS TO READ

Biskup, Agnieszka. *Understanding Global Warming With Max Axiom, Super Scientist.* Mankato, Minn.: Capstone Press, 2008.

David, Laurie, and Cambria Gordon. *The Down-to-Earth Guide to Global Warming.* New York: Orchard Books, 2007.

Gore, Al. *An Inconvenient Truth: The Crisis of Global Warming.* New York: Viking, 2007.

Hall, Julie. *A Hot Planet Needs Cool Kids.* Bainbridge Island, Wash.: Green Goat Books, 2007.

Nardo, Don. *Climate Crisis: The Science of Global Warming.* Minneapolis: Compass Point Books, 2008.

INTERNET SITES

FactHound offers a safe, fun way to find Internet sites related to this book. All of the sites on FactHound have been researched by our staff.

Here's all you do:
   Visit *www.facthound.com*
FactHound will fetch the best sites for you!

Index

About the Author

Rachael Hanel has written more than 20 nonfiction books for young readers. She specializes in history, social studies, and biography. She has degrees in history and journalism from Minnesota State University, Mankato. Hanel lives in Madison Lake, Minnesota, and is working on a memoir.